HISTORIC PHOTOS OF
NEWARK

TEXT AND CAPTIONS BY SHARON HAZARD
AND ELIZABETH HAZARD

TURNER
PUBLISHING COMPANY

Newark, a city of wide streets and tall buildings, is captured in this photograph taken from Raymond Boulevard in the 1930s.

HISTORIC PHOTOS OF
NEWARK

Turner Publishing Company
200 4th Avenue North • Suite 950
Nashville, Tennessee 37219
(615) 255-2665

www.turnerpublishing.com

Historic Photos of Newark

Copyright © 2009 Turner Publishing Company

Library of Congress Control Number: 2009922626

ISBN: 978-1-59652-538-2

Printed in China

09 10 11 12 13 14 15 16—0 9 8 7 6 5 4 3 2 1

CONTENTS

ACKNOWLEDGMENTS...VII

PREFACE VIII

RISE TO PROMINENCE
    (1860s–1899).. 1

ROBUST GROWTH IN THE NEW CENTURY
    (1900–1929) 53

HARD TIMES AND BETTER
    (1930–1960) 123

NOTES ON THE PHOTOGRAPHS 201

Amelia Earhart dedicates the new Administration Building at Newark Airport in 1935.

Acknowledgments

This volume, *Historic Photos of Newark,* is the result of the cooperation and efforts of many individuals and organizations. It is with great thanks that we acknowledge the valuable contribution of the following for their generous support:

The Library of Congress
Newark Public Library
New Jersey State Archives

PREFACE

Newark has thousands of historic photographs that reside in archives, both locally and nationally. This book began with the observation that, while those photographs are of great interest to many, they are not easily accessible. During a time when Newark is looking ahead and evaluating its future course, many people are asking, "How do we treat the past?" These decisions affect every aspect of the city—architecture, public spaces, commerce, infrastructure—and these, in turn, affect the way that people live their lives. This book seeks to provide easy access to a valuable, objective look into the history of Newark.

The power of photographs is that they are less subjective than words in their treatment of history. Although the photographer can make subjective decisions regarding subject matter and how to capture and present it, photographs seldom interpret the past to the extent textual histories can. For this reason, photography is uniquely positioned to offer an original, untainted look at the past, allowing the viewer to learn for himself what the world was like a century or more ago.

This project represents countless hours of review and research. The researchers and writers have reviewed countless photographs in numerous archives. We greatly appreciate the generous assistance of the individuals and organizations listed in the acknowledgments of this work, without whom this project could not have been completed.

The goal in publishing this work is to provide broader access to this set of extraordinary photographs that seek to inspire, provide perspective, and evoke insight that might assist people who are responsible for determining Newark's future. In addition, the book seeks to preserve the past with adequate respect and reverence.

With the exception of touching up imperfections that have accrued with the passage of time and cropping where necessary, no changes have been made. The focus and clarity of many images is limited by the technology and the ability of the photographer at the time they were taken.

The work is divided into eras. Beginning with some of the earliest known photographs of Newark, the first section records photographs through the end of the nineteenth century. The second section spans the beginning of the twentieth century through World War I and up to the beginning of the Great Depression. Section Three moves from 1930 to World War II and the postwar world the war engendered.

In each of these sections we have made an effort to capture various aspects of life through our selection of photographs. People, commerce, transportation, infrastructure, religious institutions, and educational institutions have been included to provide a broad perspective.

We encourage readers to reflect as they go walking in Newark, strolling through the city, its parks, and its neighborhoods. It is the publisher's hope that in utilizing this work, longtime residents will learn something new and that new residents will gain a perspective on where Newark has been, so that each can contribute to its future.

—Todd Bottorff, Publisher

In 1871, Stephen Crane, author of *The Red Badge of Courage,* lived at 14 Mulberry Place, the small row house with the arched entrance shown here.

Rise to Prominence

(1860s–1899)

Purchased from the Hackensack Indians in 1666, the land that would become Newark was settled by Puritans unhappy with the terms of a merger imposed by King Charles II on the colonies of New Haven and Connecticut farther east. They called the town Milford, which was changed to Newark when local government was established.

No other time in Newark's history is more important to its growth and development than the nineteenth century, during which it began to thrive. The building of the Morris Canal and the Essex Railroad in the 1830s put Newark at the center of a vital transportation route connecting the town and its products with the rest of the country. Proximity to this important transportation network placed Newark at the forefront of the Industrial Revolution. By 1840 the city had become the largest manufacturer of leather goods, and it was here that Seth Boyden perfected leather-making with the invention of shiny leather, more commonly known as patent leather. As the manufacturing of products grew, Irish and German immigrants began flocking to the city for work. The city soon experienced a spike in population, and a shift in culture. German breweries such as Ballantine and Krueger began driving the economy until, by 1880, Newark was the sixth-largest brewer of beer in the nation.

After the war, industrial advances lured curious minds to the city. Thomas Edison opened shops in 1871, spending the next five years working on improvements to the telegraph and manufacturing his innovative devices. The nation's innovators were also beginning to discover all the uses to which they could harness electric energy. In 1888, Edison competitor Edward Weston opened the Weston Electrical Instrument Company, which would grow famous for its volt meters, transformers, and other breakthrough devices. By the end of the century, the once mainly agricultural town had successfully transformed itself into a thriving, bustling city.

The progress Newark made in the 1800s was threatened by the onset of the Civil War in 1861 as a dividing line between the North and South created roadblocks to the transportation of goods. The demand for Newark's industrial prowess, however, was greater now than ever with the urgent need for goods and supplies, and Newark's economy continued to grow during the war years. During the decade, photography began to emerge from its origins in the 1830s, and it is here that the pictorial narrative of the city bequeathed by Newark's early photographers is joined.

Originally a stereograph, this image of the Morris and Essex Railroad Bridge was recorded in 1862.

As the city of Newark grew it became necessary to run it more efficiently. Incorporating the town seemed to be the answer. In 1836, the town was divided into voting districts called wards, and the citizens voted for their first city officials. This photograph shows part of the first and seventh wards, originally located on Seventh Avenue in the Italian immigrant neighborhood.

Newark in the late 1800s drew men with ideas. Here they found the mental stimulus to turn their ideas into inventions and the skilled labor to take those inventions to the marketplace. Thomas Edison was one of these men of vision. Twenty-four years old in the winter of 1871, he arrived in Newark with the title of inventor and $40,000 that Western Union had paid him to build an improved stock ticker. Needing space to manufacture 1,200 tickers immediately, Edison leased the top floor of a four-story building at 4-6 Ward Street. While in Newark, Edison began to form his core group of dreamers and craftsmen he would take with him to nearby Menlo Park to begin his "Invention Factory."

Thomas Edison opened his Ward Street plant in 1871. It was here that the mimeograph was invented in 1875.

This is one of Edison's printing telegraphs, manufactured at the Newark shops. Printing telegraphs enabled banks and brokerage firms to quickly transmit stock prices to their customers.

Home of General Philip Kearny. Nicknamed the One-Armed Devil after a bullet to the arm in the Mexican-American War ended in amputation, General Kearny is considered one of New Jersey's greatest Civil War heroes. Though deemed unfit for service, the army realized its need for experienced leaders during the Battle of Bull Run and gave him command of the New Jersey Brigade. Kearny died during battle at Chantilly in 1862. Newark claims him as their own for the summers he spent at his grandfather's home on Belleville Avenue, and a statue of the soldier stands in Military Park.

The teaching staff at the 18th Avenue School poses for a group portrait in 1880.

The original "Hallelujah Lassies," who were led by Commissioner George S. Railton to "open fire" on America, are pictured in this photograph from the files of *War Cry,* a Salvation Army publication. Lieutenant Emma Morris, later Major Emma Westbrook, was the first Lassie to be assigned to the outpost in Newark. She is pictured in the second row, at center, in 1880.

Vincent's Band and the Kemp Sisters' Wild West Show drew large crowds to Electric Park, located in the Vailsburg section of Newark, in 1889. A popular spot for picnics and outings, the amusement park was owned by the Krueger brewing family. Many residents believed the park ruined the neighborhood and it was dismantled in the 1920s.

The Charles Coe Coal Company. Coal stoves were once relied on for heating homes and businesses, which relied on delivery wagons to obtain the needed product. Homes often included coal chutes, where the coal was unloaded into basement storage areas.

The Newark Little Giants played professional baseball for the Eastern League before disbanding in the late 1880s.

Newark City Hospital's first ambulance is shown here in 1886.

In the Blizzard of 1888, heavy snowfall yields to the toil of these shovel-wielding men outside the T. P. Howell Leather Manufacturing Company.

With so many German immigrants arriving and living in Newark, beer was an important commodity. Krueger, Ballantine, and Feigenspan were some of the well-known breweries started by German families. German immigrants dominated the brewing business in Newark so much that National Brewers' Association meetings were translated into German up to 1872. Workers at the Ballantine Brewery take time out for a group shot.

Before 1900, Newark's three big department stores were Hahnes, L. S. Plaut and Company, and the original Bamberger's. Hahnes, the oldest of the three, began as a birdcage store in 1858 and expanded to selling general merchandise in the 1870s. L. S. Plaut and Company, known as the BeeHive, was founded in 1870 beside the Morris Canal. In 1923 it was purchased by Sabastian Kresge and became the well-known Kresge's Department Store. L. Bamberger and Company was founded in 1892 by Louis Bamberger and two partners, Louis M. Frank and Felix Fuld. The original Bamberger's was located on Market Street.

Members pose outside the Active Gun Club headquarters at South Orange and Munn avenues in 1890.

The Babies' Hospital was located at the corner of Bank and High streets.

This milk truck delivered fresh and sanitary milk for Dr. Coit's Babies' Hospital. "Wise Charity," went part of the hospital's creed, "Does not pauperize the poor, but helps them by adding to their resources enough money or assistance to Solve the problem."

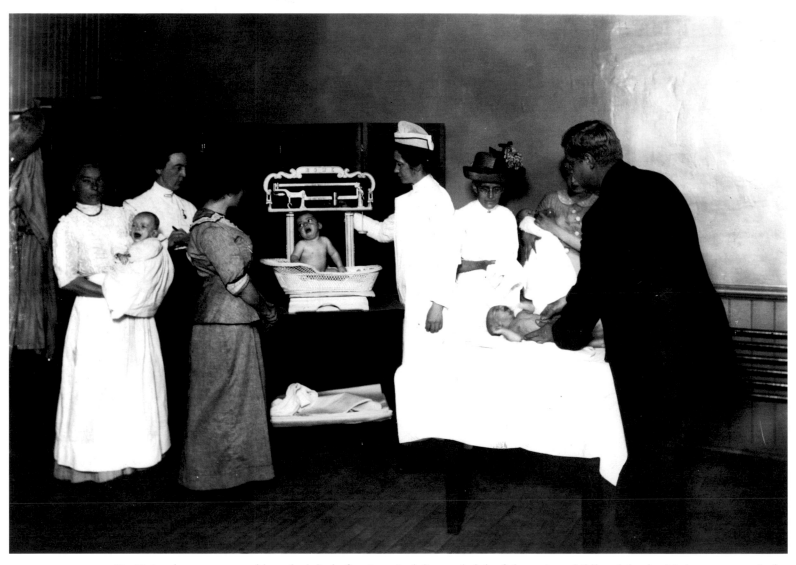

Dr. Coit, whose two-year-old son had died of an intestinal disease, led the fight against childhood deaths. He began a crusade for better infant nourishment and more sanitary methods of distributing milk, instituting a program of milk purification in 1892 and setting up "Baby Keep Well" stations throughout the city.

The nursery at Babies' Hospital. The sign on the back wall says, "There are Forty thousand babies in the City of Newark, and the Babies' Hospital treats or feeds about Two Thousand Five hundred of these infants every year."

Nurses in training in 1890. Left to right are Mrs. Luefz; Miss Lovejoy; Miss Bruckner; Miss Van Scaroth; Dr. Hickman (standing); Mr. Storz, superintendent of the hospital (seated); Miss Deheck; Miss Bramback; Mrs. Storz, matron (seated); Mill Volkemith; Miss Jade; Miss Bohlen; and Miss Gillespie.

Young ladies examine prints cataloged in the Newark Public Library in 1890. Among the images on display are the Sphinx of Egypt, an elephant, and swans on a lake.

A Washington Street School classroom is shown here around 1890. The Stars and Stripes, which features 39 stars in this image, was changing rapidly during a time when several of the western states were being admitted to the Union.

Newark youth enjoy a Christmas Day skate in 1890 on Blue Jay Swamp, now part of Branch Brook Park. Waverly Park, another popular recreational spot, was the site of New Jersey State Agricultural Society exhibitions from 1867 to 1899. Thousands would flock to the area, today known as Weequahic Park.

Gas Company workers pose outside company headquarters in 1890.

The northwest corner of Broad and Market streets in the late 1800s finds Newark's citizens pursuing their daily errands as trolleys ply the thoroughfares on rails crisscrossing the cobblestone pavement. The imposing Essex County Courthouse presides over the scene at center.

Looking west on Market Street at the famous "Four Corners" in the 1890s. Horse-drawn streetcars began service in June 1860. By the 1890s the first electric trolley cars had begun to appear on city streets.

The home of Marcus Ward and his family, at 49 Washington Street, from 1842 forward. Owner of a soap and candle–making factory at 204 Market Street, Ward grew successful as a businessman. He became governor of New Jersey in 1866 and a U.S Congressman in 1873. During the Civil War, soldiers reportedly came to the home to collect coffee beans to take back to camp.

The garden of the Ward homestead, from the back of the house facing Plane Street. The carriage house is on the left.

The Essex Hudson Gas Company was charted on March 25, 1845. In 1869, Eugene Vanderpool was named president of the company, a position he held until his retirement in 1895. The company headquarters, where this photograph was most likely taken, was located at 9 Bank Street.

A wide assortment of gas stoves are on display in the Essex Hudson Gas Company showroom, for sale to those needing a new appliance. The sign on the back wall says, "Jewell stoves are the best."

Tiffany and Company began manufacturing sterling silver in a new plant located at 820 Highland Avenue in north Newark in 1896. The building, complete with turrets and bricks imported from England, looked more like a castle than a factory. The building survives today as an apartment complex.

John Cotton Dana, public librarian, museum director, president of the American Library Association, and today member of the Library Hall of Fame, was director of the Newark Public Library from 1902 to 1929. He founded the Newark Museum in 1909, directing purchases of art that included examples of the Ashcan School.

Members of the Atlanta Wheelmen, a cycling club, pose in front of Borcherling Mansion on Park Place ready to start a race in 1893. Among the contestants are Ernest Miller, Charles Swain, Amzi Dodd, William V. Belknap, and "Count" Olozaga. The large-wheeled penny farthings in view here were an early design of the bicycle, which would assume its modern form during the 1890s.

A bicycling group from the Ironbound section enjoys an outing in 1893.

Hand-carved by John Campbell of Belleville, the statue of a fireman waves to the city from atop the mansard-style roof of the Firemen's Insurance Building at Broad and Market streets sometime in the 1890s. The handsome edifice was erected in 1868 and demolished in 1909, to be replaced by a newer, 16-story structure, the new home of the Prudential Insurance Company. Amid the hustle and bustle of trolleys and wagons in view here are numerous businesses, among them the Newark Theatre, Ludlow's Pool and Billiard Table manufacturing, and Hallet and Davis Piano Company inside the Niagara Building.

The Morris Canal passed under Broad Street and Center Market on its way to Jersey City. At 90 miles long, the canal stretched from Newark to Phillipsburg, becoming vital to the transportation of goods during the onset of the Industrial Revolution. Pictured is Lock 17 East in Newark, as it looked in 1894.

Immense cloth awnings like the two adorning the Public Service Building here, helped to reflect the harsh rays of the sun in cities across the United States, shading and cooling Americans inside in the days before air conditioning.

Mutual Benefit Insurance Company was located inside this ornate Victorian structure in the commercial district on Broad Street. Mutual Benefit was founded in 1845 by Robert L. Patterson and 11 business associates, including grocers, merchants, and manufacturers.

Employees of Bamberger's department store pose for a photograph in 1893. At 131 Market Street, Bamberger's massive flagship store covered an entire city block. Employees of Bamberger's Department Store pose for a photograph in 1893, the year the business began. The original store was located at 147 Market Street. In 1912, Louis Bamberger built a new store at the corner of Broad and Market streets that occupied an entire block and employed more than 2,800 people. Macy's would purchase Bamberger's in 1929, continuing the operation under the Bamberger name, as well as the Thanksgiving Day parade begun by Bamberger's in 1926 that would become famous as the Macy's parade beloved by Americans today.

Theodore P. Howell of the
Newark Fire Department poses
for a photographer.

44

Engine Company Number 7 flaunts a state-of-the-art horse-drawn steam pumper for this group shot recorded in 1894.

Department Chief McDermott makes ready his team of horses, shown here harnessed to pull a steam pumper engine from the fire house and into the street.

Members of Newark's first bicycle squad pose for a group shot in 1898. From left to right are officers Letzeller, Peter J. McKenna, Fox, Harry Stillman, Templeton, Sergeant Harry Bitz, William Murphy, Sam Brown, Charles Lindner, and Frederick Kuhn.

The Newark Academy was an all-boys school that provided education to the sons of Newark's wealthy. This photograph of the class of 1897 identifies those pictured by surname. They are, from left to right (at rear), Smith, Hand, Lord, Reisen, Heller, Carrington, Kinney; (third row) Frey, Miriam, Jones, Frazer, Swift, Williams, Headley, Reeves; (second row) Prout, Schurman, Drake, Doc Farrand, Thompson, Knorr, Thurston; (front row) Hendricks, Plum, Garabrant, Casebold, and McCabe.

Posing for a group shot here are the national, state, county, and city rowing champions from the Institute Boat Club. Bottom row, left to right, are Dr. John Pardue, James H. Reilly, Owen E. Fox, William Kiley, Valentine Lockmyer, and Edward Kerns. Second row: Edward Feuerherm, John Lupten, John Lawrence, John O'Brien, Thomas H. Knowles, Henry Schwertfuehrer, and James Noonan. Top row: Walter Healy, John Burke, John J. Murphy, Al Fitzpatrick, Francis Sullivan, and Cornelius McManus.

The Newark High School graduating class of 1899.

Biederman's Boys Band poses with the Stars and Stripes in this proud display of patriotism.

The Great Blizzard of 1899 swept across the Eastern Seaboard in February, dropping more than a foot of snow in Newark.

ROBUST GROWTH IN THE NEW CENTURY

(1900–1929)

Newark really began to take shape as a city at the turn of the century. Electric trolley cars replaced horse-drawn carriages. Multiple-floor department stores such as Bamberger's, Hahne's, and Kresge's took shoppers away from the small specialty stores. Big insurance companies and factories filled the skyline. The streets were bustling with activity, so much so that the corner of Broad and Market streets, the city's main thoroughfare, became known to the world as the Four Corners, the country's busiest intersection. To offer citizens a release from the daily noise and traffic of the city, famed landscape designer Frederick Law Olmsted created a haven for city dwellers with Branch Brook Park, the first county park to be opened for public use in the United States. During both world wars, the Army would use the park as a training base for soldiers. The Morris Canal, which ran alongside the park, was to be abandoned, becoming the site for Newark's subway.

Education played an important role in the development of Newark as well, and prominent schools cropped up throughout the 1900s. Newark today is home to Rutgers University Law School, St. Benedict's Preparatory School, and countless vocational schools. A wide range of athletic events coincided, and the local parks played host. When Newark celebrated its 250th anniversary in 1916, a track and field competition held at Weequahic Park to help observe the milestone broke several records.

With the entry of the United States into World War I in 1917, education would take less priority. Like the nation as a whole, Newark was called into action and all citizens took heed. Port Newark was transformed into an army base and more than 20,000 Newark residents sailed for the war fronts overseas. Construction of the Newark Shipyard began in September 1917 and within nine months the first ship for the war effort had been built and launched—an unparalleled example of American ingenuity and know-how at its finest.

Newark became a hub of transportation when the city opened the first major airport in the metropolitan area in October 1928. With international and national flights leaving on a daily basis, by 1929 it had become the world's busiest commercial airport. The terminal made a great impact on the city's economy, bringing both tourism and jobs to the area. But the economy would be challenged in the years to come as the nation faced the Great Depression.

This rooftop view of Newark offers a bird's-eye view of the city's main business and government buildings.

At the turn of the century, leather tanning remained one of Newark's main industries. This 1900 photograph shows workmen in the Neider Tannery. At one time Newark was the nation's leading leather-producing city.

A fire at Broad and Cedar streets destroyed Snyder's Department Store in 1900.

Before trolleys brought in more shoppers and department stores saw the need to supply a wider variety of goods, most shops on Broad Street were small and specialized.

Food and other commodities were sold on Newark's busy streets, now increasingly traversed by the automobile.

Newark's first department store opened in 1858 at the corner of Broad Street and Central Avenue. Pocketbook maker Julius Hahne opened it as a birdcage store and later expanded to carry four floors of general merchandise. The store would not close until 1986. This window display features fashions for the new century and its preoccupation with the Gibson Girl, a stylized rendering of the ideal in femininity created by artist Charles Dana Gibson.

Broad and Market streets.

In 1900, Bamberger's offered their patrons many amenities, including valet parking.

The early 1900s were a happy time in Newark, but across the ocean the storm clouds of war were soon to be gathering. Pedestrians are shown here in Military Park downtown.

The Prudential Insurance Company building on the corner of Broad and Market streets held a Lackawanna Railroad ticket office at street level. When the structure opened, at 16 stories it was New Jersey's tallest skyscraper. It would later be home to F. W. Woolworth Five and Ten Cent Store.

Located at Washington Park, the American Insurance Company Building sported Corinthian columns, pillars, balustrades, and pilasters. At front, Christopher Columbus is depicted in bronze. The statue was dedicated to the famous Italian explorer in 1927.

Hahne's promotes Mother's Week in May 1902, where "extraordinary inducements in boys and girls wearables" offer blouses for 29 cents.

In the opening game of the Eastern League played April 21, 1910, Newark competes against Rochester.

Another view of the field on opening day, April 21, 1910. One trusts that Hetzel's had cemented and painted any leaks in this roof before game day.

Indiana native Bill Rariden played for the Newark Peppers in 1915. He batted 40 runs in during the season, and his batting average for the season was .270.

Shown here in 1910, Lew McAllister played catcher in the Newark Eastern League.

Patrons arrive for a day of shopping at Bamberger's Department Store in 1913.

Rooftop panorama of Newark as the city looked in 1912.

Phineas Jones was a nationally recognized wheelwright. His company manufactured the first tires for Henry Ford's automobiles as well as the heavy wheels needed to transport circus wagons owned by Ringling Brothers. This photograph was taken in 1915.

The Central High School football team for 1913: Standing left to right are Robert L. Smith, manager; James Alveron, assistant coach; Harry Bennett, full back; Jacob Frank, full back; Ed Nevins, center; George Smith, right tackle; Harold Engelberger, right half back; William Schmidt, right half back; Albert Erler, guard; Jay Bauer, quarterback; Ray Krout, quarterback and end; John Flockhart, tackle; Harry Sargent, coach. Kneeling are Charles Hopkins, end; Frank Simmonds, tackle; J. Gordon Cryer, guard; Jacob Lesser, guard; George Ritchie, end; Chester Backer, end; William Brohrn, guard; Elber Powell, end; Elmer Dickson, guard; Charles Schoeber, end; Charles Mutter, tackle. Seated are Albert Kaplansky, guard; Israel Greenberg, center; Sidney Safier, quarterback; Charles Allen, quarterback; Chester Wagner, halfback; Harry Bossett, halfback; Norman Becker, halfback; Harry DeGroot, tackle; and William Brogan, end.

Members of the Newark Boating Club pose for a club photograph on deck around 1915.

Nereid Boat Club members prepare for a race. Pictured in the craft are, left to right, Edgar King, Roxbury McCormack, and Bill Bradshaw.

Standing at 163 Howard Avenue, newsie Max Schwartz, eight years old, and his older brother, Jacob Schwartz, hawk newspapers until ten o'clock at night in December 1909. Employed by the National Child Labor Committee, Lewis Hine traveled the nation in these years photographing underprivileged, working children in an effort to end the practice of child labor. Losing government patronage in the 1930s for lack of interest in his work, Hine himself grew impoverished, dying penurious in 1940.

Lewis Hine photographed seven-year-old Tony and a friend hawking newspapers in Newark one late afternoon in November 1912.

The National Turners Gymnastics Club performs in Weequahic Park on July 4, 1915.

A. E. Ward of Chicago wins the 100 yard dash in 1916, running the straightaway in an even 10 seconds. The Amateur Athletic Union's track and field competition was held at Weequahic Park as part of the celebration of Newark's 250th anniversary.

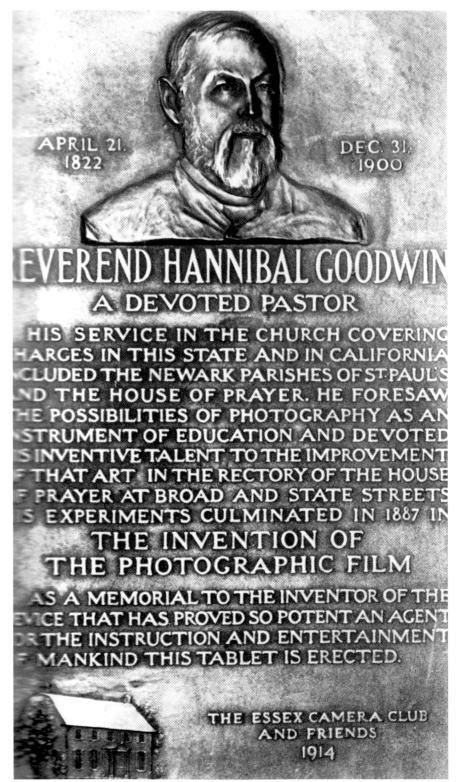

APRIL 21. 1822

DEC. 31. 1900

EVEREND HANNIBAL GOODWIN

A DEVOTED PASTOR

HIS SERVICE IN THE CHURCH COVERING
HARGES IN THIS STATE AND IN CALIFORNIA
CLUDED THE NEWARK PARISHES OF St PAUL'S
ND THE HOUSE OF PRAYER. HE FORESAW
HE POSSIBILITIES OF PHOTOGRAPHY AS AN
STRUMENT OF EDUCATION AND DEVOTED
S INVENTIVE TALENT TO THE IMPROVEMENT
F THAT ART IN THE RECTORY OF THE HOUSE
F PRAYER AT BROAD AND STATE STREETS
S EXPERIMENTS CULMINATED IN 1887 IN
**THE INVENTION OF
THE PHOTOGRAPHIC FILM**
AS A MEMORIAL TO THE INVENTOR OF THE
VICE THAT HAS PROVED SO POTENT AN AGENT
R THE INSTRUCTION AND ENTERTAINMENT
F MANKIND THIS TABLET IS ERECTED.

THE ESSEX CAMERA CLUB
AND FRIENDS
1914

Episcopal priest Hannibal Goodwin successfully patented celluloid photographic film in 1898, after 11 years of interference by Eastman Kodak. In his quest to illustrate the scriptures for Sunday school students, the rector of the House of Prayer in Newark had wanted to make negatives out of something other than glass. Goodwin died of injuries sustained in a street accident in 1900, just as the film company he founded was set to begin production of the film he invented.

These men wait in line to enlist for service in what was known as Newark's Own. Patriotism knew no age or status barriers in this photograph taken in March 1917, on the eve of America's entry into a worldwide conflict that had originated in Serbia in summer 1914 with the assassination of an Austrian archduke.

The first ship built at the Newark Shipyards, christened the *Agawan,* slid off the ways into Newark Bay on Memorial Day 1918, while the crowd cheered and some commented, "It floats." The nine months that had elapsed between the start of construction of the shipyards and the launching of the *Agawan* is a feat that remains unmatched in the annals of shiplore. The industrial might of the United States would soon begin to be appreciated by the enemy abroad.

Goings on at the Newark Shipyard during the World War I era. As the war effort ramped up, the yard became the second-largest shipyard in the nation, employing as many as 25,000 men.

Trains leaving Central Station are loaded with soldiers as well-wishers line the platform. More than 20,000 citizens of Newark would leave home to engage in the conflict abroad.

Newark women march up Broad Street to show their support for the doughboys fighting overseas.

Female volunteers attend evening classes to learn wireless telegraphy, to replace male operators being called to duty overseas.

Newark's women dance with soldiers on leave at the National Service League on Broad Street in 1918.

Officers and recruits share a meal in the mess hall in 1918.

Newark welcomes home its servicemen, shown here on Broad Street at war's end. With victory in World War I, America's role as the leading world power was beyond dispute.

Some of Newark's young newsboys hawk newspapers around 1920.

In 1920, these women trudge through snow and slush to City Hall to place before Mayor Raymond a resolution calling for purchase and sale by the city of needed food.

WOR Radio Station was started in the radio department of Bamberger's in 1922 as a marketing tool to sell more radios. John Gambling became the on-air personality. Three generations of the Gambling family would eventually serve as WOR hosts.

94

This youngster listens to the radio from a family living room in the Ritz Apartments in 1923.

The Newark Horse Show took place on May 2, 1925. The saddle class division, left to right, includes Mrs. C. Leroy Wood on Fifty-Five, Mrs. H. S. Broadbent on Worrisome, Miss Marjorie Ross on Elite, Miss Mary Matthews on Dutch, Miss Jean Matthews on Quick Silver, Miss Ida Cosgrove on Jennie Glazier, Miss Margie Wood on Dutchess, and Virginia Boycott on Mary Glazier.

Opening day at Newark Athletic Stadium, October 24, 1925.

Workers pour concrete for the foundation of offices at the Newark airport in the 1920s. Beginning service in 1928, the air terminal would become the busiest in the world until New York's LaGuardia opened in 1939.

The scene at the dedication of the Administrative Building at Newark Airport.

The Prudential Insurance Company employed more than 9,000 people. This image was recorded in 1925 when a group of workers stopped traffic outside the company headquarters on Broad Street.

The Newark Philharmonic Band performs for concert-goers at Branch Brook Park on July 19, 1926, around eight-thirty that evening.

J. Massey Rhind's statue of George Washington is located in Washington Park, on Broad Street and Washington Place. The monument shows the general taking leave of his army at Rocky Hill, Washington's final headquarters during the Revolutionary War. This is one of three Newark monuments commissioned by Amos Van Horn, a wealthy local merchant.

Wars of America was third in the series of commissions financed by Amos Van Horn. Its presence dominates Military Park downtown. This photograph shows the sculptor, Gutzon Borglum, inspecting his 42-foot-long masterpiece, which includes 42 human figures and 2 horses representing all major conflicts involving the United States up to World War I. Borglum is best-known for his work at Mount Rushmore in South Dakota.

Essex County Courthouse, at Springfield Avenue and Market Street, was designed by Cass Gilbert in a modified Renaissance style. It was built of granite and marble and features a central dome.

In the plaza of the Essex County Courthouse is the famous seated bronze statue of Abraham Lincoln by Gutzon Borglum. The statue was unveiled in 1911, and to this day children love to climb up and sit on Lincoln's lap.

An antiquated horse-drawn steam pumper belches smoke as firemen attempt to extinguish a blaze at Baumann and Lee's Furniture Store in 1926.

John Hardin, President of Mutual Life Insurance Company, pauses from work at his desk in 1927.

Shown here in 1927, the dining room in the new Mutual Benefit Insurance Building had a seating capacity of 700.

Originally known as Waverly Park, this recreational area has long been known as Weequahic Park. These young men are enjoying a game of ice hockey on one of the many frozen ponds in the park in 1927.

Two steelworkers pose on the framework of the New Jersey Bell Telephone Company Building at 540 Broad Street. When it was built in 1928, it rose 20 stories into the air and was topped by a soft orange light that illuminated Washington Park across the street. The Newark Public Library is visible below, and in the distance the imposing Sacred Heart Cathedral, two well-known landmarks for the two aging daredevils to gaze down upon.

Lightning Electric Company employees pose for the camera outside their offices in 1929. The founders of the company, Ben Nadelberg and Albert Richman, are 9th and 13th from the right, respectively.

Newark mayor Thomas Raymond greets Mr. and Mrs. Herbert Hoover at the South Street station in 1928. Hard at it on the presidential campaign trail, Hoover had arrived in Newark to address voters.

A colony of several hundred Chinese immigrants settled Chinatown just off Mulberry Street. An area of homes and businesses was known as Mulberry Arcade until the 1920s, when federal raids forced inhabitants to relocate. At left, the Shanghai Restaurant advertises "real Chinese food."

Essex County Girls Vocational School joined the lengthy roster of buildings constructed during the building boom of the 1920s.

Students learn how to dye fabric at Essex County Vocational School in 1930.

Groundbreaking for Sacred Heart Grammar School is under way around the late 1930s.

G. Pizza Grocery Store, at 157 14th Street, sold Italian specialty grocery items.

A game of bocce is in progress in a neighborhood in the northern sector of Newark. The community was home to Americans of Italian descent.

The Department of Labor training service conducts an English language class for Italian immigrants at the Y.M.C.A. in 1929. Knowing English would enable new arrivals to qualify for citizenship.

Essex County Hall of Records, at High Street and 13th Avenue, was erected in 1927. It was a giant in a district of small stores and brick and frame houses. Near the entrance is a group of carved stone figures depicting the purchase of this site from the Lenni Lenape Indians.

The American Insurance Company, shown here in 1929, was located just across the street from Military Park.

Veteran lock tenders John H. Lackey, John Vorhees, and John J. McFaul (left to right) pose in the late 1920s behind the balance beam used to open and close the lock gates that controlled the water level in a nearby lock.

HARD TIMES AND BETTER

(1930–1960)

Because of Newark's location, it was always the idea of transportation that encouraged its growth. The building of Newark Airport was a catalyst to strengthening the economy on the eve of the Great Depression and during the depression years. Constructed on open swampland just outside the city, this project provided jobs for many people. Laborers from every trade were needed. Planners and architects were employed and raw materials were purchased. Newark Airport opened in 1928 adding prestige to the city, and in 1935, Amelia Earhart dedicated the new Administration building.

As the Great Depression unfolded, all the industrial gains Newark had built itself on came to a standstill as manufacturing slowed and jobs vanished. It was an everyday sight to see men in lines hoping to get a job or at least a decent meal. In response, the federal government launched a barrage of radical programs known as the "New Deal," among them the Emergency Relief Administration and Works Progress Administration. President Roosevelt himself came to Newark and spoke at the Robert Treat Hotel with the goal of strengthening the morale of the people. Few places were harder hit by the Great Depression than Newark, in large measure for its dependence on manufacturing and shipping.

World War II had a great impact on Newark, erasing the depression's record levels of unemployment, still 17 percent across the nation in 1939. Men were off to war overseas and women took over the jobs usually done by men in factories and manufacturing plants and sent care packages to the soldiers. Food, clothing, and gasoline were rationed, and Victory gardens blossomed as wives, mothers, and sweethearts waited anxiously for the war to end. Victory over Japan came in August 1945, ending the war and launching the United States in the postwar era as a superpower and leader of the free world.

After the war, Newark faced a housing shortage, addressed by the Newark Housing Authority with affordable housing for the GIs and their growing families. A poor economy, housing problems, and weak municipal government began to define the next few decades in the city's history. The troubling times would culminate in the 1960s with the racially fueled riots that gripped the country. Newark suffered great devastation. The years ahead would be a time of challenge for the city and its residents as it sought to rebuild. Like the cherry blossoms in Branch Brook Park that keep coming back every spring, Newark is a town that continues to find ways to rejuvenate.

Washington Street in 1930. The crash on Wall Street had occurred the preceding year, but the worst of its repercussions for the nation and the residents of Newark were only beginning.

Students hone their skills in the art of hair-dressing at Essex County Vocational School in 1930.

At Fawcett School of Art, later known as the Newark School of Fine and Industrial Arts, young women work to acquire skill at the difficult art of drawing. Long hours of practice yielded results, but not every student had the aptitude that would lead to high proficiency in the craft.

Pennsylvania Station. Adding to Newark's reputation as a transportation center, Pennsylvania Railroad Station opened in 1935 for use by railroad trains, trolleys, and tube trains. Its construction was a joint venture between the railroad and the city of Newark. Designed by the architectural firm McKim, Meade, and White, the neoclassical building featured a facade of limestone piers and glass.

Clothing is distributed on Avon Avenue in 1933 as part of a relief effort for those in need.

Trucks load up to distribute food during the Great Depression.

Caputo's Flower Shop, at 167 Sheffield Street, did enough business during the Great Depression to keep its doors open.

Automobiles and trolleys alike plied Orange Street in the early 1930s. By 1938 all trolley cars had been retired downtown. Newark and cities across the nation were beginning to substitute buses for use in public transportation.

Works Progress Administration workers complete road repair work.

The Great Depression had a grave impact on big cities like Newark. In 1933, these out-of-work mechanics are employed at small construction projects in the workroom of the Civil Works Authority state headquarters at 70 Washington Place.

Prizes are awarded for Essex County's Emergency Relief Administration Gardens on September 28, 1934.

Emergency Relief Administration headquarters in Newark was a busy place on January 11, 1934.

City Hall on Broad Street between Greene and Franklin streets was built in the French Renaissance style in 1906. The four-story limestone structure with its ornately decorated gold dome houses the city's administrative offices. The structure has undergone restorative work, which was completed the year of its centennial birthday in 2006.

Last surviving veterans of the Civil War are honored on Memorial Day in front of City Hall in 1934.

National Prohibition lasted from 1920 to 1933, and its enforcement put a blight on brewery businesses across the country, including those in Newark. This photo shows four employees of the Krueger Brewery loading the first barrels of beer to be produced after repeal of the Eighteenth Amendment on April 7, 1933.

The Great Depression left families cold, hungry, and sometimes homeless. This photo shows unemployed men seeking jobs at the Newark Armory in 1933.

The Salvation Army delivers food to a needy family, one of so many in Newark hurt by the Great Depression, in 1933.

The superintendent of Kresge Department Store presents a trophy to Don Hawley, winner of the men's single's tennis tournament in Branch Brook Park, on September 24, 1932. The event was sponsored by Kresge's.

Other tennis match winners in 1932 are presented trophies by the general manager of Kresge Department Store.

Mary Stillwell Edison, Thomas Edison's first wife, died at the age of 29 in 1884. She was buried in Mount Pleasant Cemetery. Edison himself would live to pursue his life's work until 1931. His son Charles, born in West Orange, became the 42nd governor of New Jersey in the election of 1940.

Members of the Barringer High School girl's fencing team. Left to right are Joan Matheke, Josephine Mancinelli, and Jeam Finger, posing for the camera on March 5, 1935.

One sign on this Depression-era storefront church identifies the meetinghouse as Sweet Bethel Missionary Baptist Church. Another sign invites the community to "Come and help us to save one soul."

The Savannah Market on West Kinney Street offers fresh produce for sale to neighborhood customers somtime in the 1930s.

At Oriental Street, the *Miles Standish* is scrapped in 1935.

Prince Street, located between Spruce Street and Springfield Avenue, was where Jewish merchants set up shop indoors and on the sidewalk selling everything from produce to clothing. In the 1930s, synagogues lined the six-block-long street.

Among the shops lining Central Avenue in the 1930s are the Stumpp and Walter garden supply store, Eno's Restaurant, and Donna Beauty Salon. Up to the 1960s and even in the hard times of the Great Depression, most Americans considered suits, dresses, and hats the appropriate standard in attire when out and about. Everyone made the effort to look his best.

Airplanes would become an important part of Newark and the nation's defense in World War II. The Casey Jones School of Aeronautics trained pilots and military personnel. Pictured in this cockpit is the first president of the school, Casey Jones himself.

By 1934, the Newark Airport was a busy place. In this view, a TWA plane at left and an American Airlines biplane at right rest on the tarmac.

Passengers find ways to pass the time in the waiting room at Newark Airport in the 1930s.

Music and dancing at Newark's Skateland, 1930s style.

Home to countless theaters and clubs, Newark figured prominently in the jazz era. Jazz legend Sarah Vaughan and the great comedian, actor, and band leader Jackie Gleason both got their start at venues in the city.

Divident Hill is located in Weequahic Park. It is the highest point in the park, and a tablet marks the scene of the meeting held in 1668 at which the founders of Newark and Elizabethtown reached a boundary agreement.

John R. Hardin, president of Mutual Benefit Life of Newark, stands on the left of E. E. Rhodes in 1930s.

The Post Office, Essex County Courthouse, and the steeple of a church make up a typical city scene in Newark in 1934.

South Park Presbyterian Church, at 1035 Broad Street, was built in 1855 at a cost of $27,000, becoming one of New Jersey's finest Greek Revival churches. Abraham Lincoln gave a brief address here in 1861. Vacant for many years, the building burned in 1992, and today only the facade remains standing. Efforts to restore the facade began in 2008.

Trinity Episcopal Church is located at 608 Broad Street overlooking Military Park. During the Revolutionary War the church was used as a hospital. The original structure was destroyed by fire in 1804 and was rebuilt in 1810. The church became the cathedral for the Newark Diocese in 1942. In 1966 it was united with St. Philip's Episcopal Church, becoming Trinity and St. Philip's Cathedral in 1992.

Blessed Sacrament Church is located on Van Ness Place and Clinton Avenue.

Shown at the Robert Treat Hotel in Newark, President Franklin D. Roosevelt addressed a meeting of the National Emergency Council to organize federal relief agencies during the Great Depression. Pictured at the January 18, 1936, meeting along with the president is Charles Edison, at the time State Director of the Emergency Council. As the 1930s began drawing to a close, the massive federal relief effort that had characterized the decade faced sobering statistics: the average unemployment rate, which climbed to 16 percent in 1931 and 25 percent by 1933, hovered at a depressing 19 percent in 1938.

Market Street in the 1930s. The facade of Star Electrical Supply Company, which did business in a turn-of-the-century building with few distinguishing features, was redesigned in 1936 with all the latest in modern design: neon signage, an electric clock, and rear-lit glass panels. The new design was intended as "built-in" advertising for Star's leading products: all the latest in electric light fixtures.

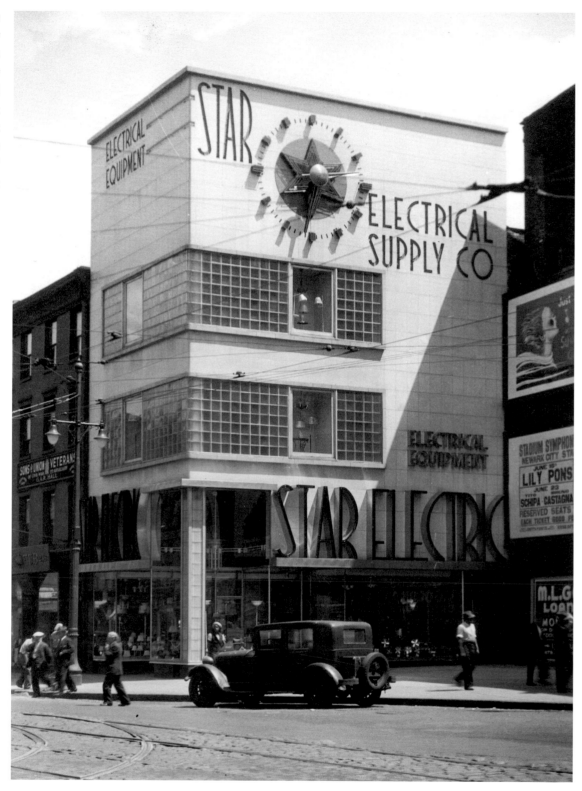

The dedication of Harrison Street near the entrance to the Pulaski Skyway.

Taverns and tenement dwellings line a street near the Post Office around the turn of the decade.

Northwest Passage starring Spencer Tracy and *Private Detective* starring Jane Wyman were playing at the National Theater here in 1940, the same year that Wyman married another rising star by the name of Ronald Reagan. Theaters of the era were offering patrons air-conditioned spaces, a strong inducement at a time when home air-conditioning was prohibitively expensive and enjoyed by few Americans.

The Prudential Building's unique design featured turrets and curved archways. The building was demolished in 1958.

Newark Housing Authority public housing of the 1940s. Many of the buildings built by the Authority were brick structures, six to eight stories tall, and built around an inner courtyard.

A lower-middle-income area, Down Neck was chosen as the site of the Chellis-Austin Apartments, built in 1931 by the Prudential Insurance Company as an experiment in medium-cost housing for residents of moderate income. A children's playground was part of the concept.

This scene at Pennington Court finds children busy at play in the 1940s.

Inner courtyards like this one were the hub of everyday life for residents of public housing in 1944. This courtyard was located at 57 Sussex Street.

Newman's Grocery Store is doing a brisk business here in the 1940s.

By the 1940s, Port Newark was a leading terminal for imported cars and lumber. Stevedores are working here to unload bundles of lumber from the decks of the cargo vessel *Texmar*.

Four young ladies receive the first contribution for the Newark USO from the general chairman of the Newark United Service Organization and from a vice-president of Bamberger's Department Store. The USO was created in 1941 by the Y.M.C.A., the Salvation Army, and other groups as a private, nonprofit organization to serve the recreational needs of on-leave servicemen in the U.S. armed forces. During World War II, the USO opened more than 3,000 clubs at home and abroad, offering movies, dancing, religious counsel, and free coffee and doughnuts to armed forces personnel.

Essex County Red Cross women meet in 1945 in Glen Ridge to knit socks for soldiers serving in World War II.

Three housewives with husbands in the service sort empty aluminum, tin, and lead tubes, which will be melted down at the Newark plant of the Tin Salvage Institute. In addition to recovering tin, a substantial volume of lead was reclaimed in this manner for use in war industries.

The dedication of McCarter Highway on December 17, 1943, was recorded by more than one camera crew.

The Newark Eagles played professional baseball at Ruppert Stadium in the Negro National League from 1936 to 1948, winning the league's World Series in 1946 in an upset against the Kansas City Monarchs.

Baseball fans attend a game at Ruppert Stadium on Wilson Avenue. The Newark Bears played here from 1926 to 1949.

Admitting office for Kenney Memorial Hospital, today home to New Salem Baptist Church. The hospital was founded and funded in 1927 by Dr. John Kenney, who donated the hospital to the community on Christmas Eve 1934.

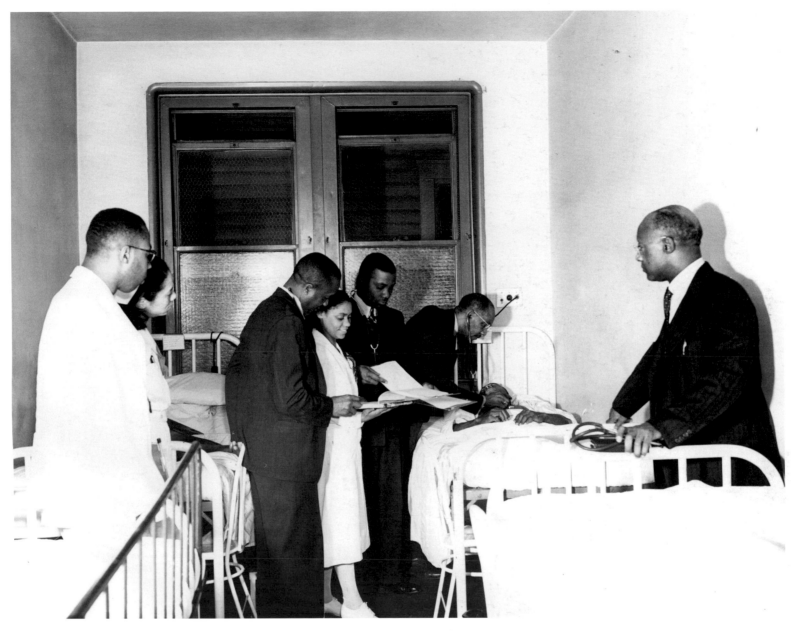

A patient is examined in the Men's Ward at Kenney Memorial–Community Hospital.

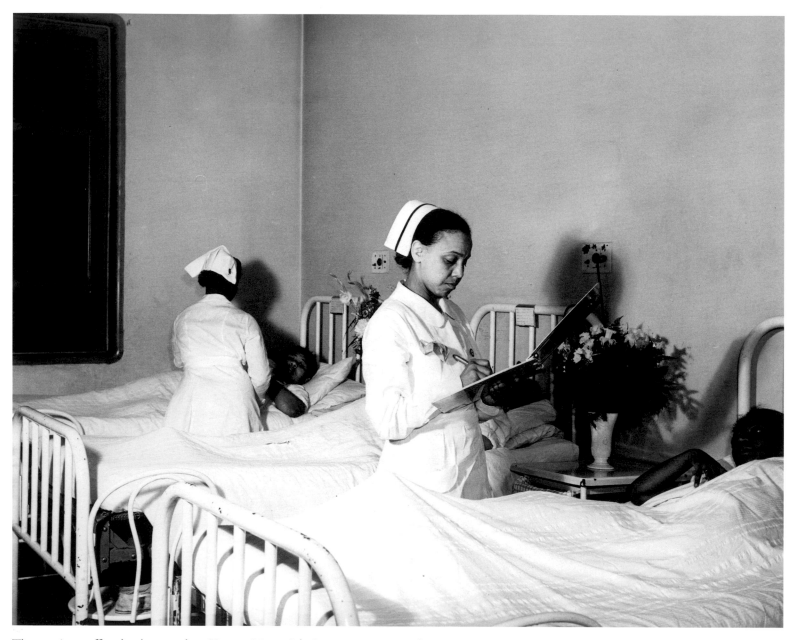

The nursing staff make the rounds at Kenney Memorial–Community Hospital.

Veterans pose for a photo at the 50th Anniversary Banquet of the Battery A Veterans Association, held in 1945 at the Newark Athletic Club.

Dedication ceremonies are under way on May 17, 1947, for the new Stickel Memorial Bridge.

186

A crowd of pleased citizens listen to an official address at the Stickel Memorial Bridge dedication.

A tranquil vista and pleasant surroundings at Branch Brook Park.

Jackson and Perkins garden company was founded in Newark in 1872 by Charles Perkins and A. E. Jackson to specialize in wholesale strawberry plants and grapevines. The company began growing and hybridizing roses before the turn of the century, and in the twentieth century would become the world's foremost purveyor of the flower. One of the grower's rose fields is shown here in 1947.

Newark Airport opened in October 1928 on 2,100 acres in Elizabeth and Newark. In its earliest days the airport was the nation's busiest airfield and remains the 10th busiest today. The terminal is shown here on a day in the 1940s.

The baggage claim area at Newark Airport in 1953.

Newark Airport was renamed Newark Liberty International Airport after the terrorist attacks of September 11, 2001, in which United Airlines Flight 93 departed gate A17 bound for San Francisco. When the plane was hijacked by Al Qaeda operatives and rerouted toward targets in Washington, D.C., passengers led by Todd Beamer fought the terrorists for the cockpit. The plane crashed in a field near Shanksville, Pennsylvania, far short of its target.

Stone lions stand sentry above the front entrance to the original Prudential Building on Broad Street.

Group Shot of the Newark National Guard's 119th Fighter Squadron in 1955. The 119th was organized on September 17, 1917, as the 119th Aero Squadron at Langley Field, Virginia, for participation in World War I.

An automobile is unloaded at Port Newark in 1958.

On June 26, 1957, Miss Audrey Kisonak of Westfield, along with builders and construction foreman Joe Pizatelli, polishes the Mutual Benefit Seal removed from the floor of the old building for reinstallation inside the insurance company's new building.

The First Baptist
Peddie Memorial
Church meetinghouse,
at Broad and
Fulton streets, was
built in 1890. The
congregation was
organized on June 6,
1801, baptizing several
new believers that day
in the Passaic River.

The new Prudential Insurance building on Broad Street towers above the street in the early 1960s.

Cherry blossoms at Branch Brook Park in 1960. The park's Cherry Blossom Festival remains an annual event enjoyed by many.

Notes on the Photographs

These notes, listed by page number, attempt to include all aspects known of the photographs. Each of the photographs is identified by the page number, photograph's title or description, photographer and collection, archive, and call or box number when applicable. Although every attempt was made to collect all data, in some cases complete data may have been unavailable due to the age and condition of some of the photographs and records.

II RAYMOND BOULEVARD PANORAMA
New Jersey State Archives
WPA

VI AMELIA EARHART AT NEWARK AIRPORT
New Jersey State Archives
WPA

X STEPHEN CRANE HOME ON MULBERRY PLACE
New Jersey State Archives
WPA

2 MORRIS AND ESSEX RAILROAD BRIDGE
Library of Congress
LC-DIG-stereo-1s01473

3 EARLY NEWARK
Library of Congress
LC-DIG-stereo-1s01474

4 THOMAS EDISON
Library of Congress
LC0USZ62-98067

5 EDISON'S WARD STREET PLANT
Newark Public Library
10.260.2

6 EDISON PRINTING TELEGRAPH
Newark Public Library
stock_ticker

7 GENERAL KEARNY HOME
Library of Congress
LC-DIG-stereo-1s01475

8 18TH AVENUE SCHOOL TEACHING STAFF
Newark Public Library
21

9 THE ORIGINAL "HALLELUJAH LASSIES"
Newark Public Library
36

10 ELECTRIC PARK PERFORMERS, 1889
Newark Public Library
41

11 CHARLES COE COAL COMPANY
Newark Public Library
72

12 NEWARK LITTLE GIANTS BASEBALL TEAM
Newark Public Library
66

13 CITY HOSPITAL'S FIRST AMBULANCE
Newark Public Library
Newark, Image 27,
Newark City Hospital First
Ambulance

14 BLIZZARD OF 1888
Newark Public Library
35

15 BALLANTINE BREWERY WORKERS GROUP SHOT
Newark Public Library
52

16 HAHNES, L. S. PLATT, AND BAMBERGER'S
Newark Public Library
05

18 GUN CLUB MEMBERS
Newark Public Library
64

19 BABIES' HOSPITAL
Newark Public Library
25

20 BABIES' HOSPITAL MILK TRUCK
Newark Public Library
27

21 DR. COIT AND HOSPITAL STAFF WITH PATIENTS
Newark Public Library
24

22 BABIES' HOSPITAL NURSERY
Newark Public Library
26

23 NURSES IN TRAINING, 1890
Newark Public Library
23

24 **PUBLIC LIBRARY PRINT ROOM**
Newark Public Library
13

25 **WASHINGTON STREET SCHOOL CLASSROOM**
Newark Public Library
47

26 **CHRISTMAS DAY SKATE ON BLUE JAY SWAMP**
Newark Public Library
29

27 **GAS COMPANY WORKERS**
Newark Public Library
49

28 **BROAD AND MARKET STREETS, 1890S**
Library of Congress
LC-USZ62-77362

29 **FOUR CORNERS**
Newark Public Library
03

30 **MARCUS WARD HOME**
Newark Public Library
40

31 **MARCUS WARD HOME NO. 2**
New Jersey State Archives
HABS
39

32 **ESSEX HUDSON GAS COMPANY HEADQUARTERS**
Newark Public Library
48

33 **GAS STOVES FOR SALE**
Newark Public Library
50

34 **TIFFANY AND COMPANY MANUFACTURING PLANT**
Newark Public Library
Newark, Image 19, Tiffany Factory

35 **JOHN COTTON DANA**
Newark Public Library
30

36 **ATLANTA WHEELMEN CYCLING CLUB GROUP SHOT**
Newark Public Library
63

37 **SOCIAL OUTING, 1893**
Newark Public Library
37

39 **FIREMEN'S INSURANCE BUILDING**
Newark Public Library
01

40 **MORRIS CANAL**
Newark Public Library
Newark, Image 45 morris canal

41 **PUBLIC SERVICE BUILDING FACADE**
Newark Public Library
Newark, Image 48-A, public service bldg.

42 **MUTUAL BENEFIT INSURANCE COMPANY BUILDING**
Newark Public Library
Newark, Image 55-A mutual benefit bldg. 1800s

43 **BAMBERGER'S DEPARTMENT STORE EMPLOYEES**
Newark Public Library
04

44 **FIREMAN THEODORE HOWELL**
Newark Public Library
14

45 **ENGINE COMPANY NO. 7**
Newark Public Library
12

46 **FIRE CHIEF McDERMOTT**
Newark Public Library
15

47 **POLICE OFFICERS, 1898**
Newark Public Library
44

48 **NEWARK ACADEMY CLASS OF 1897**
Newark Public Library
28

49 **INSTITUTE BOAT CLUB CHAMPIONS**
Newark Public Library
57

50 **NEWARK HIGH SCHOOL CLASS OF 1899**
Newark Public Library
Newark, Image 39, Newark High graduating class

51 **BIEDERMAN'S BOYS BAND**
Newark Public Library
42

52 **BLIZZARD OF 1899**
Newark Public Library
38

54 **ROOFTOP VIEW OF THE CITY**
Library of Congress
pan 6a07798

55 **NEIDER TANNERY WORKMEN**
Newark Public Library
Newark, Image 29, neider tannery

56 **FIRE AT BROAD AND CEDAR STREETS**
Newark Public Library
16

57 **BROAD STREET COMMERCE**
Newark Public Library
Newark, Image 57, small specialty stores

58 **BUSY DOWNTOWN STREET**
Newark Public Library
22

59 **HAHNE'S DISPLAY WINDOW**
Newark Public Library
33

60 **SPRINGFIELD AND HIGH STREETS**
Newark Public Library
02

62 **PEDESTRIANS IN CITY PARK**
Newark Public Library
Newark, Image 2, strolling in military park

63 **INSURANCE COMPANY SKYSCRAPER**
Library of Congress
LC-USZ62-132004

64 **PARK PLACE SKYSCRAPER**
New Jersey State Archives
WPA
American Insurance Company 832C

65 HAHNE'S DISPLAY WINDOW NO. 2
Newark Public Library
32

66 EASTERN LEAGUE OPENING GAME FOR 1910
Library of Congress
pan 6a36470

67 EASTERN LEAGUE OPENING GAME NO. 2
Library of Congress
pan 6a36463

68 NEWARK PEPPERS' PLAYER BILL RARIDEN
Library of Congress
LC-DIG-ggbain-17159

69 THE EASTERN LEAGUE'S LEW MCALLISTER
Library of Congress
LC-DIG-nclc-03820

70 BAMBERGER'S PARKING
Newark Public Library
06

71 ROOFTOP PANORAMA
Library of Congress
pan6a14039

73 PHINEAS JONES WHEEL WORKS
Newark Public Library
45

74 CENTRAL HIGH SCHOOL FOOTBALL TEAM, 1913
Newark Public Library
62

75 NEWARK BOATING CLUB MEMBERS, 1915
Newark Public Library
60

76 NEREID BOAT CLUB REGATTA PREPARATIONS
Newark Public Library
08

78 LEWIS HINE NEWSIES
Library of Congress
LC-DIG-nclc-03356

79 LEWIS HINE NEWSIES NO. 2
Library of Congress
LC-DIG-nclc-03820

80 NATIONAL TURNERS GYMNASTICS CLUB EXHIBITION
Newark Public Library
61

81 250TH ANNIVERSARY TRACK AND FIELD COMPETITION
Library of Congress
LC-DIG-ggbain-22756

82 HANNIBAL GOODWIN PLAQUE
Newark Public Library
Newark, Image 31, hannibal goodwin

83 WORLD WAR I RECRUITS
Newark Public LibraryNewark, Image 3, WWI, waiting in line

84 NEWARK SHIPYARDS IN WARTIME
Library of Congress
LC-DIG-ggbain-25860

85 NEWARK SHIPYARDS IN WARTIME NO. 2
Library of Congress
LC-DIG-ggbain-25866

86 CENTRAL STATION GOOD-BYES
Newark Public Library
Newark, Image4, trains leaving station

87 PARADE ON THE HOMEFRONT
Newark Public Library
Newark, Image 5, women marching

88 WIRELESS TELEGRAPHY VOLUNTEERS
Newark Public Library
Newark, Image 6, female volunteers

89 DANCE FOR SOLDIERS ON LEAVE
Newark Public Library
Newark, Image 7, WWI dancing with soldiers

90 SHARING A MEAL IN THE MESS HALL
Newark Public Library
70

91 A WELCOME HOME FOR SERVICEMEN
Newark Public Library
Newark, Image 7-A, soldiers return home, WWI

92 NEWSBOYS IN 1920
Library of Congress
LC-DIG-nclc-04057

93 RESOLUTION FOR MAYOR RAYMOND
Library of Congress
LC-USZ62-96179

94 JOHN GAMBLING (THE FIRST) AT WOR RADIO
Newark Public Library
46

95 YOUNG RADIO FAN
Library of Congress
LC-USZ62-93073

96 NEWARK HORSE SHOW, 1925
Newark Public Library
59

97 ATHLETIC STADIUM OPENING DAY
Newark Public Library
65

98 NEWARK AIRPORT CONSTRUCTION
New Jersey State Archives WPA
Newark- Administration Building Newark Airport pouring concrete 171

99 AIRPORT DEDICATION
New Jersey State Archives WPA
Newark- Dedication Administration Building at Newark Airport 807

100 PRUDENTIAL INSURANCE EMPLOYEES
Newark Public Library
Newark, Image 8, prudential workers outside off

101 NEWARK PHILHARMONIC BAND IN CONCERT
Newark Public Library
30

102 RHIND STATUE OF WASHINGTON
New Jersey State Archives WPA
George Washington Statue

103 **BORGLUM'S WARS OF AMERICA SCULPTURE**
Library of Congress
LC-USZ62-127430

104 **ESSEX COUNTY COURTHOUSE**
New Jersey State Archives
WPA
Essex County Courthouse
833A

105 **STATUE OF LINCOLN AT THE COURTHOUSE**
New Jersey State Archives
WPA
Abraham Lincoln at
Courthouse 951H

106 **BLAZE AT BAUMANN AND LEE'S FURNITURE STORE**
Newark Public Library
17

107 **MUTUAL LIFE PRESIDENT JOHN HARDIN**
Newark Public Library
67

108 **DINING ROOM AT MUTUAL BENEFIT INSURANCE BUILDING**
Newark Public Library
68

109 **ICE HOCKEY AT WEEQUAHIC PARK**
Newark Public Library
56

110 **AGING STEELWORKER DAREDEVILS**
Newark Public Library
Newark, Image 30
steelworkers top telephone co.

111 **LIGHTNING ELECTRIC COMPANY EMPLOYEES**
Newark Public Library
Newark, Image 32, lightning
elec. co.

112 **HERBERT HOOVER WITH MAYOR RAYMOND**
Library of Congress
LC-USZ62-102521

113 **OFF MULBERRY STREET**
New Jersey State Archives
WPA
Mulberry Arcade Chinatown

114 **ESSEX COUNTY GIRLS VOCATIONAL SCHOOL**
New Jersey State Archives
Con and Econ
Essex County Girls
Vocational School

115 **DYEING FABRIC AT THE VOCATIONAL SCHOOL**
Newark Public Library
19

116 **GROUNDBREAKING FOR CATHEDRAL**
Newark Public Library
73

117 **G. PIZZA GROCERY STORE**
New Jersey State Archives
WPA
G. Pizza Grocery Store

118 **GAME OF BOCCE IN PROGRESS**
New Jersey State Archives
WPA
Italian Bocce Court

119 **ENGLISH LANGUAGE CLASS FOR ITALIAN IMMIGRANTS**
Library of Congress
LC-USZ62-9309

120 **ESSEX COUNTY HALL OF RECORDS**
New Jersey State Archives
WPA
Essex County Hall of Records

121 **AMERICAN INSURANCE COMPANY**
Newark Public Library
Federal Court House, exterior

122 **VETERAN LOCK TENDERS**
Newark Public Library
Newark, Image 46 morris
canal lock tenders

124 **WASHINGTON STREET, 1930**
New Jersey State Archives
Telephone Building

125 **PRACTICING COIFFURE AT THE VOCATIONAL SCHOOL**
Newark Public Library
20

126 **ART STUDENTS AT FAWCETT SCHOOL OF ART**
Newark Public Library
Newark, Image 19, fawcett
school of art

127 **PENNSYLVANIA RAILROAD STATION**
New Jersey State Archives
WPA
Pennsylvania Railroad Station
(Penn Station) 956A

128 **AVON AVENUE RELIEF EFFORT**
New Jersey State Archives
WPA
Newark- Clothing
Distribution Avon Ave. 159

129 **TRUCKS FOR RELIEF EFFORT FOOD**
New Jersey State Archives
WPA
Newark-O & W Trucks 414

131 **THE SCENE AT CAPUTO'S FLOWER SHOP**
New Jersey State Archives
WPA
Caputo's Florist

132 **ORANGE STREET, 1930s**
New Jersey State Archives
WPA
470 Orange Street

133 **WPA ROAD CREW WORK PROJECT**
New Jersey State Archives
WPA
WPA workers doing road
repairs in Newark

134 **WPA CARPENTRY PROJECTS**
New Jersey State Archives
WPA
Newark- Mechanics in
work shop of CWA at 20
Washington Place 43

135 **EMERGENCY RELIEF GARDEN PRIZES**
New Jersey State Archives
WPA
Newark-Awarding prize for
Essex Co. ERA Gardens at
Newark Airport 572

136 EMERGENCY RELIEF ASSOCIATION HEADQUARTERS
New Jersey State Archives
WPA
Newark-Newark ERA Office
450

137 CITY HALL
New Jersey State Archives
WPA
City Hall

138 HONORING THE LAST SURVIVING CIVIL WAR VETERANS
Newark Public Library
34

139 THE END OF PROHIBITION
Newark Public Library
51

140 NEWARK'S UNEMPLOYED
Newark Public Library
54

141 SALVATION ARMY FOOD DELIVERY
Newark Public Library
53

142 KRESGE TENNIS MATCH AWARD
Newark Public Library
09

143 KRESGE TENNIS MATCH AWARD NO. 2
Newark Public Library
10

144 EDISON GRAVE MONUMENT
Newark Public Library
75

145 BARRINGER HIGH SCHOOL FENCERS
Newark Public Library
55

146 DEPRESSION ERA STOREFRONT CHURCH
New Jersey State Archives
WPA
Store Front Church

147 SAVANNAH MARKET ON WEST KINNEY STREET
New Jersey State Archives
WPA
Newark- Savannah Market
West Kinnet Street 706A

148 SCRAPPING THE MILES STANDISH
New Jersey State Archives
WPA
Newark- Oriental Street
Wrecking Miles Standish 505

149 PRINCE STREET MERCHANDISING
New Jersey State Archives
WPA
Prince Street Newark 1269A

150 CENTRAL AVENUE STOREFRONTS
New Jersey State Archives
WPA
31 Central Avenue

151 CASEY JONES IN THE COCKPIT
Library of Congress
LC-USZ62-114597

152 NEWARK AIRPORT, 1934
New Jersey State Archives
WPA
Newark-Newark Airport
Dedication 804

153 NEWARK AIRPORT WAITING ROOM
Newark Public Library
Newark, Image 14, airport
waiting room

154 SKATELAND DANCERS
New Jersey State Archives
WPA
Rug cutters at the Skateland

155 JAZZ ERA CLUBBERS
New Jersey State Archives
WPA
Afro Club Newark

156 DIVIDENT HILL MARKER
New Jersey State Archives
WPA
Divident Hill, Weequahic
Park 820 B

157 JOHN HARDIN AND E. E. RHODES
Library of Congress
14578u

158 THE POST OFFICE
New Jersey State Archives
WPA
Post Office & Court House
Building

159 SOUTH PARK PRESBYTERIAN CHURCH
Library of Congress
HABS NJ,7-NEARK,7-1

160 TRINITY EPISCOPAL CHURCH
New Jersey State Archives
HABS
NJ-34 Trinity Episcopal
Church Newark

161 BLESSED SACRAMENT CHURCH
New Jersey State Archives
WPA
Blessed Sacrament Church
810A

162 PRESIDENT ROOSEVELT ADDRESSING THE NATIONAL EMERGENCY COUNCIL
Newark Public Library
Newark, Image 55, pres.
roosevelt

163 STAR ELECTRICAL SUPPLY
New Jersey State Archives
WPA
STAR Electrical Supply
Newark 831A

164 DEDICATION OF HARRISON STREET
New Jersey State Archives
DOT
Dedication Newark Harrison
Rt. 25A Detour 1943

165 POST OFFICE BACK STREET
New Jersey State Archives
WPA
Slums near Post Office 287D

167 THE NATIONAL THEATER
New Jersey State Archives
WPA
National Theatre Newark

168 PRUDENTIAL INSURANCE BUILDING
Newark Public Library
Untitled-5

169 **PUBLIC HOUSING IN THE 1940S**
Library of Congress
LC-G612-T01-49427

170 **CHELLIS-AUSTIN APARTMENTS PLAYGROUND**
New Jersey State Archives
WPA
Children's Playground at
Prudential Apartments

171 **CHILDREN AT PENNINGTON COURT**
New Jersey State Archives
WPA
Newark Housing Authority
Pennington Court 1479K

172 **SUSSEX STREET COURTYARD**
Newark Public Library
untitled-7

173 **SCENE AT NEWMAN'S GROCERY STORE**
New Jersey State Archives
WPA
Newman's Grocery Store

174 **PORT NEWARK CARGO**
New Jersey State Archives
WPA
Port Newark 1043A

175 **USO ORGANIZERS**
Newark Public Library
Newark, Image 52 uso.
WWII

176 **RED CROSS SOCK KNITTERS**
Newark Public Library
71

178 **METAL SORTERS FOR THE WAR EFFORT**
Newark Public Library
Untitled-1

179 **MCCARTER HIGHWAY DEDICATION**
New Jersey State Archives
DOT
Dedication McCarter
Highway Newark 1943

180 **THE NEWARK EAGLES**
Newark Public Library
Newark, Image 72-B, newark
eagles

181 **FANS AT BASEBALL GAME**
Newark Public Library
Newark, Image 72-D,
baseball field, wilson av.

182 **KENNEY HOSPITAL ADMISSIONS OFFICE**
New Jersey State Archives
WPA
Community Hospital-
Admitting Office

183 **KENNEY HOSPITAL MEN'S WARD**
New Jersey State Archives
WPA
Community Hospital-Nurses

184 **KENNEY NURSES MAKING THE ROUNDS**
New Jersey State Archives
WPA
Community Hospital-Nurses

185 **VETERANS GROUP SHOT**
New Jersey State Archives
NJNG
SDENG010-C042

186 **STICKEL MEMORIAL BRIDGE DEDICATION**
New Jersey State Archives
DOT
Dedication Rt. 25 A Stickel
Memorial Bridge Newark

187 **STICKEL MEMORIAL BRIDGE DEDICATION NO. 2**
New Jersey State Archives
DOT
Dedication Rt. 25 A Stickel
Memorial Bridge Newark
1949

188 **VISTA AT BRANCH BROOK PARK**
New Jersey State Archives
WPA
Brank Brook Park 949A

189 **JACKSON AND PERKINS ROSE GARDENS**
Newark Public Library
Untitled-6

190 **NEWARK AIRPORT, 1940S**
New Jersey State Archives
Con and Econ
Newark Airport, no date

191 **NEWARK AIRPORT BAGGAGE CLAIM, 1953**
New Jersey State Archives
Con and Econ
Newark Airport Baggage
Claim 1953

193 **NEWARK AIRPORT TARMAC**
New Jersey State Archives
Con and Econ
Newark Airport Passangers
unloading from American
Airlines

194 **FRONT ENTRANCE TO PRUDENTIAL BUILDING**
Newark Public Library
Untitled-4

195 **NATIONAL GUARD'S 119TH FIGHTER SQUADRON**
New Jersey State Archives
NJNG
SDENG010-A178

196 **UNLOADING AUTOMOBILE AT PORT NEWARK**
New Jersey State Archives
Con and Econ
Norton Lilly Terminal at Port
Newark 1958

197 **MOVING THE MUTUAL BENEFIT SEAL**
Newark Public Library
69

198 **FIRST BAPTIST PEDDIE MEMORIAL CHURCH**
Library of Congress
HABS NJ,7-NEARK,33-2

199 **BROAD STREET, 1960S**
New Jersey State Archives
Con and Econ
New Prudential Insurance
Building

200 **CHERRY BLOSSOMS AT BRANCH BROOK PARK**
New Jersey State Archives
Con and Econ
Cherry Blossoms at Branch
Park 1960